COOL CATS

Egyptian Maus

by Domini Brown

BELLWETHER MEDIA • MINNEAPOLIS, MN

BLASTOFF!
2
READERS

Note to Librarians, Teachers, and Parents:

Blastoff! Readers are carefully developed by literacy experts and combine standards-based content with developmentally appropriate text.

Level 1 provides the most support through repetition of high-frequency words, light text, predictable sentence patterns, and strong visual support.

Level 2 offers early readers a bit more challenge through varied simple sentences, increased text load, and less repetition of high-frequency words.

Level 3 advances early-fluent readers toward fluency through increased text and concept load, less reliance on visuals, longer sentences, and more literary language.

Level 4 builds reading stamina by providing more text per page, increased use of punctuation, greater variation in sentence patterns, and increasingly challenging vocabulary.

Level 5 encourages children to move from "learning to read" to "reading to learn" by providing even more text, varied writing styles, and less familiar topics.

Whichever book is right for your reader, Blastoff! Readers are the perfect books to build confidence and encourage a love of reading that will last a lifetime!

This edition first published in 2016 by Bellwether Media, Inc.

No part of this publication may be reproduced in whole or in part without written permission of the publisher. For information regarding permission, write to Bellwether Media, Inc., Attention: Permissions Department, 5357 Penn Avenue South, Minneapolis, MN 55419.

Library of Congress Cataloging-in-Publication Data

Brown, Domini.
  Egyptian Maus / by Domini Brown.
    pages cm. – (Blastoff! Readers. Cool Cats)
  Summary: "Relevant images match informative text in this introduction to Egyptian maus. Intended for students in kindergarten through third grade"– Provided by publisher.
  Audience: Ages 5-8.
  Audience: K to grade 3.
  Includes bibliographical references and index.
  ISBN 978-1-62617-310-1 (hardcover : alk. paper)
  1. Egyptian mau–Juvenile literature. I. Title.
  SF449.E39B76 2016
  636.8'2–dc23

                          2015028713

Printed in the United States of America, North Mankato, MN.

Table of Contents

Egyptian maus are one of the oldest **domestic** cat **breeds**.

These short-haired cats are the only breed with naturally spotted **coats**.

They are called maus for short. *Mau* means "cat" in Egyptian.

These cats have **agile**, medium-sized bodies.

Egyptian maus have a **royal** past. The breed may be more than 3,000 years old!

Egypt

N
W E
S

Ancient art shows spotted cats with **pharaohs** in Egypt. They were honored pets.

In 1956, a Russian princess brought maus to New York. Her cats made the breed popular in the United States.

Today, maus are loved
in homes all over!

Mau coats are silver, **bronze**, black, or **smoke**.

Egyptian Mau Coats

silver

bronze

black

smoke

All maus have dark spots on their backs and legs. Their bellies are light.

These cats look wild. Dark stripes mark their cheeks and foreheads. Mau eyes are **gooseberry** green.

Egyptian Mau Profile

large ears

gooseberry-green eyes

spotted coat

Weight: 6 to 14 pounds (3 to 6 kilograms)

Life Span: 15 to 20 years

Fast Moves

Egyptian maus have loose belly skin and long back legs. They can take long **strides** to run fast.

Maus are the fastest domestic cats. They can reach 30 miles (48 kilometers) per hour!

These cats are quick and smart when they play. They chase feathers and toy mice.

They will **pounce** without warning!

Family Love

Egyptian maus are family cats. They follow their owners around the house.

Some maus like shoulder rides!

Glossary

agile—able to move quickly and easily

ancient—from long ago

breeds—types of cats

bronze—yellowish brown

coats—the hair or fur covering some animals

domestic—animals that are not wild and are kept as pets

gooseberry—a sour berry that is a clear, yellowish green color

pharaohs—rulers of ancient Egypt

pounce—to suddenly jump on something to catch it

royal—related to kings and queens

smoke—a coat that is light with dark tips; a smoke coat looks like dark fur.

strides—the lengths between steps when walking or running

To Learn More

AT THE LIBRARY

Landau, Elaine. *Egyptian Maus Are the Best!*
Minneapolis, Minn.: Lerner Publications Co., 2011.

Sexton, Colleen A. *The Life Cycle of a Cat.*
Minneapolis, Minn.: Bellwether Media, 2011.

Wheeler, Jill C. *Egyptian Mau Cats.* Minneapolis,
Minn.: ABDO Pub. Co., 2012.

ON THE WEB

Learning more about
Egyptian maus is as
easy as 1, 2, 3.

1. Go to www.factsurfer.com.

2. Enter "Egyptian maus" into the search box.

3. Click the "Surf" button and you will see a
   list of related web sites.

With factsurfer.com, finding more
information is just a click away.

Index

The images in this book are reproduced through the courtesy of: Sarah Fields Photography, front cover, pp. 4-5, 11, 13 (top left), 15, 19; Krissi Lundgren, pp. 6, 8; Gerard Lacz/ Rex/ REX USA, p. 7; Werner Forman Archive/ Glow Images, p. 9; Ron Kimball/ Kimball Stock, p. 10; Juniors/ SuperStock, p. 12; Mikkel Bigandt, p. 13 (top right); kuban_girl, p. 13 (bottom left, bottom right); Tbowerman, p. 14; Lisa Beattie, pp. 16-17; Zack Alexander/ Photoshot, p. 18; Julia Remezova, p. 20; Alex Milan Tracy/ Sipa USA/ Newscom, p. 21.